THE READING ACTIVITY HANDBOOK

Purposeful reading responses to enrich your literacy programme

SHEENA CAMERON

William Collins' dream of knowledge for all began with the publication
of his first book in 1819. A self-educated mill worker, he not only enriched
millions of lives, but also founded a flourishing publishing house.
Today, staying true to this spirit, Collins books are packed with inspiration,
innovation and practical expertise. They place you at the centre of a
world of possibility and give you exactly what you need to explore it.

☼ Collins. Do more.

© Sheena Cameron 2004
Sheena Cameron asserts her moral rights to be identified as the author of this work

This edition first published in the UK by Collins 2004
An imprint of HarperCollins*Publishers*
77 – 85 Fulham Palace Road
Hammersmith
London
W6 8JB

Original edition published by Reed Publishing, New Zealand
This edition is published by arrangement with Reed Publishing (NZ)

Browse the complete Collins catalogue at
www.collinseducation.com

10 9 8 7 6 5 4 3 2 1

ISBN 0 00 720029 3

British Library Cataloguing in Publication Data
A Catalogue record for this publication is available from the British Library

Printed and bound in China

Contents

Acknowledgements

I would like to thank the following people:

Ben Hope for the character grid organiser on page 31

Kylie Bracey for the story map on page 35

Sophie Villers for the author portrait on page 59

Allanah Mackintosh for the character portrait and web on page 30, the character writing on page 32, the reward poster on page 42, and the storyboard on page 14

Adam Stewart for the certificate on page 48 and the book review on page 54

Miguel Valero for the certificate on page 48

Finn Hopley for the story retell on page 68

Dylan Russell for the word prediction on page 18

Ira Neuenschwander for the character epilogue on page 32

Hayley Cradock for the character epilogue on page 32

Emma Heaps for the character writing on page 32

Sara Metz for the character letter on page 32 and the narrative outline on page 53

Rae Sanders for the 'True, false, I'm not sure' response on page 62

Debra Michaelides and Veronica van der Straaten for the myths and legends book assignment on page 55

John McCaffery for the 'Pick a card' activity on page 67 and photocopy master discussion stems on pages 91, 92 and 93

My sister Jane Prezepiorka for the bottle person idea on page 29, the story cube idea on page 49, and photo setting idea on page 47; and for her enthusiasm and encouragement

Linda Cheeseman of Green Bay Primary School for her patience and flexibility and for allowing me to work with her talented students

Margaret Aikman for her professional knowledge, encouragement and sharp editing eye

Jennifer Mair for her support and advice

Jenny Howitt for her enthusiasm and encouragement

And finally my wonderful husband, James, for his patience and good advice, and for taking our son, Sam, out on many all-day adventures so I could get some work done!

Introduction

Why use reading response activities?

While it is true that not all reading requires a response, in the real world of the classroom, teachers know that in order to meet the learning needs of individuals and small groups, the rest of the class needs to be occupied.

Providing students with opportunities to engage in purposeful reading responses has many benefits. These include:

- allowing teachers to work with individuals and small groups
- creating opportunities to observe and monitor students' comprehension
- providing authentic reading, writing, talking and creative experiences for students
- producing quality work that students value.

Who is this book designed for?

This book is designed for teachers at all levels of primary/elementary and intermediate/middle school wanting to:

- introduce their students to a wide variety of text-appropriate reading responses
- encourage independence and create opportunities for choice
- enrich and extend their literacy programme
- save time and energy in the planning process.

How will these responses benefit my students?

The responses in this book will benefit your students by:

- providing opportunities for student choice, which increases student motivation and engagement
- deepening levels of comprehension, by requiring them to return to the text for different purposes
- enabling them to make personal connections with literature
- developing independence and positive self-image as a reader.

How do the responses fit into my literacy programme?

The responses could be used before, during and after shared, guided or whole class reading sessions. It would be helpful to introduce some of the responses, such as how to construct a sociogram or Venn diagram to compare characters, at the beginning of the year in a whole class reading session. This would provide an introduction to a response that could be built on during reading sessions at a later date.

Many responses are not ends in themselves and could naturally lead to work in other areas of the curriculum. For example, a grid organiser could be used as a planning framework for a science report, or completing a plus, minus, interesting chart could lead to a discussion about a particular issue.

Students will require varying levels of support. For some students, much demonstration and modelling will be required. Initially it may be appropriate to just model the response and have no expectation of any input from the students. While they are learning a new response, have students work with a partner or in small groups of three or four students so that responsibility for the task is shared. Individual students can then attempt the response independently with some support provided by the teacher. An example of this guided approach is the book review outline in the photocopy master section of this book. The student works independently but within a framework. Finally, the student will assimilate the response into his or her repertoire and be able to complete it independently. It is vital that students are given the support appropriate to their level to set them up to succeed. It is also important that students are given many opportunities to share their completed work to demonstrate it is valued.

What texts could I use?

- Graded reading material
- Picture books
- Novels
- Poetry
- Newspaper and magazine articles
- Trade books

How do I use this book?

This book is designed as a resource book of ideas to be used when planning literacy sessions. Some responses are brief and one-off. For example, 'Best word' (see page 20) is an oral activity that could be used as a five-minute reading starter. Other responses may span longer periods of time and be taken to a high level of publication. For example, a student could create a detailed shoebox diorama and a published report to go with it that could take two weeks or more to complete. Obviously the number and type of responses will differ depending on the text, your purpose, and the needs of the students.

The book is divided into six chapters, each one focusing on different categories of responses. Many responses fit into more than one category so links to similar responses are provided at the beginning of each chapter. Each response includes student learning outcomes to assist you in planning appropriately for the needs of your students. These are written in the blue boxes in the top right-hand corner of each response. Photocopy master (PM) sheets provide additional support for some tasks. The Descriptive words chart (PM 19, page 94) could be photocopied onto coloured paper and laminated for use as a classroom resource. 'Your ideas' pages are included at the end of each chapter for you to add your own notes and ideas.

Making collections of genre types such as reports, factual and personal recounts, narrative, procedural, and minimal text genre types such as tickets, stamps, pamphlets and business cards, will make the task of modelling the specific language features of each genre easier. Collections could be made in file boxes, scrapbooks, clear file folders or resealable plastic bags. Collections of samples of students' work to use as exemplars can also become a valuable on-going teacher resource, which can be used to inspire high quality work.

When students become proficient at using a variety of responses, they are able to take responsibility for choosing the way they would like to respond to a text. Students themselves could use this handbook.

The ideas in this book are starting points. Adapt them to make them yours and, most importantly, have fun and enjoy your students' creativity!

Chapter 1

Locating and organising information

Other responses that include locating and organising information are:

- Predict and check chart
- Sociogram
- Venn diagram
- Character grid organiser
- Excitement chart
- Character web
- Character rating chart
- Narrative outline
- True, false, I'm not sure
- Drawing for comprehension
- Checklist
- Reward poster
- Brochure

1   Grid organiser

This grid organiser supports student learning by providing a structure to collect and organise information from factual or narrative text. Initially, it may be appropriate for the student to learn only how to retrieve information from a completed grid. They could then learn how to collect information under prescribed headings and eventually devise their own headings to collect information.

Once students are familiar with the use of this organiser, the teacher may use unfilled grids to assess prior knowledge on a topic before a unit of work or afterwards to assess information learned.

This structure could be also used as a framework to plan a piece of writing such as a factual report.

Grid organiser for endangered New Zealand sea birds				
Bird	**Maori name**	**Area found**	**Food**	**Number of eggs laid**
Northern royal albatross	Toroa	Chatham Islands, Taiaroa Head, Otago	Fish	1
Yellow-eyed penguin	Hoiho	Campbell, Auckland and Stewart islands, Southland, Otago	Fish and small squid	2
Reef heron	Matuku moana	On most rocky shores	Small crabs, fish	3
New Zealand dotterel	Tuturi-whatu	North Cape to Kawhia and East Cape. Stewart Island	Crustacea, shellfish	4

2   Consequences chart

An appropriate event or concept is taken from the text. The students use information from the text plus their prior knowledge to predict the consequences of a particular event occurring. This structure could be also used as a framework to plan a piece of writing.

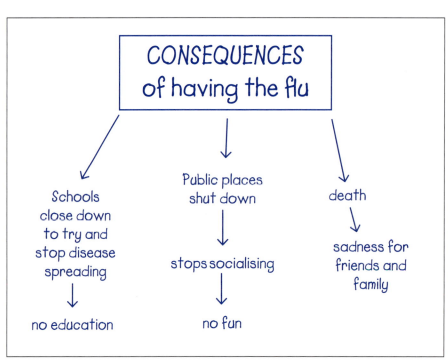

3 Timeline

Students construct a timeline of events for a specific time in the text or for the whole text.

This can be done using words, pictures or both. A timeline is also a useful framework to support the student to retell the story or as an outline for a piece of writing. As an activity at the beginning of the year, have the students construct a personal timeline. It can be very revealing to see what the children perceive as the important events in their own lives.

Timeline for

Amos and Boris

by William Steig

- Amos starts to build his boat
- Provisions the boat
- Sets sail
- Amos rolls off his boat
- Spends the night in the sea
- Meets Boris
- Boris takes him back to land
- Hurricane Yetta strikes
- Boris is stranded on the beach
- Amos finds Boris
- Elephants rescue Boris
- The two friends say goodbye

4 Before and after chart

Students record their prior knowledge about a topic in the 'before' web.

After reading the text, they complete the 'after' web, adding the information they have learned. References to pages and paragraphs where information was found is also noted. A brief summary may be written using information from the two webs.

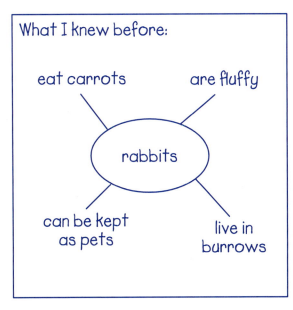

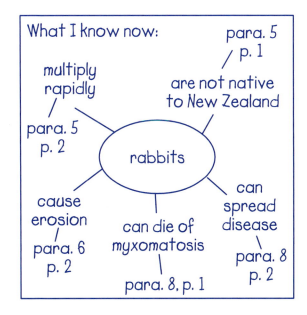

5 Y chart

Y charts can be used to explore feelings and issues associated with characters or themes within a text. Use the photocopy master PM 1 on page 74. Students write the issue or feeling in the centre, and ideas are then recorded under the headings of 'Feels like', 'Looks like' and 'Sounds like'.

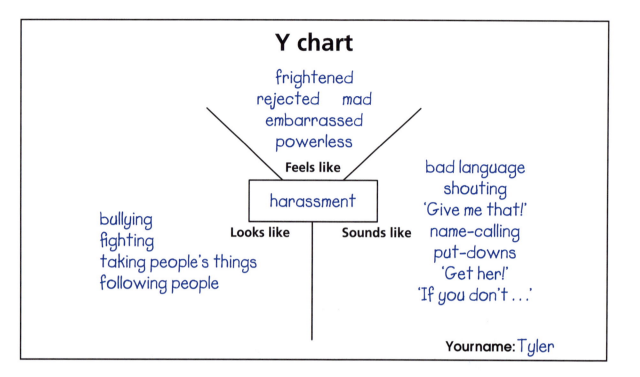

6 Flow chart

STUDENT OUTCOMES
- **Developing ability to locate and sequence key ideas**
- **Developing comprehension through in-depth reading**

Student identifies key ideas in the text, then sequences them chronologically. Words, pictures or a combination of both may be used.

7 Wall story

In a small group, students co-operatively retell the story with the teacher acting as scribe. The story can be retold in its original form or as an innovation on the text. The teacher divides the story into an appropriate number of sections for the number of students in the group and assigns each student a section to illustrate. The text and pictures are then collated and displayed on the wall or hung across the room. Later the story may be taken down and made into a shared book. An audiotape could also be recorded to create an independent reading resource.

Based on a traditional New Zealand Maori legend.

8 Circular story

A circular story is a simplified version of the wall story idea. Draw a large circle on a piece of paper then divide the circle into segments so each child in the reading group will have a segment. Cut out the segments and give one to each student. Assign each student a section of the story to summarise and illustrate. The segments are then glued onto a larger sheet of paper in chronological order, to form a circle again.

AN AUSTRALIAN LEGEND
RETOLD BY WARATAH GROUP

Based on a traditional Australian Aboriginal legend.

9 Storyboard

Students use a grid of eight squares as a framework to retell a story using words, pictures or a combination of both. Use the photocopy master PM 2 on page 75. The storyboard could also be used to plan a video sequence or a comic strip based on the story or events related to it. This framework can also be used as a support for oral retelling of the story.

Based on *Bad Girls* by Jacqueline Wilson

10 Survey

Students in a reading group develop a survey related to an issue in the text. Surveys could be administered to class, syndicate, parents or caregivers. Findings are then collated and a statement prepared to summarise results.

Green Bay School Recycling Survey

Dear Parents and Caregivers

We have been reading an article about recycling.

Can you please complete this survey to help us gather information about the recycling habits of families in our school?

We appreciate you taking the time to complete our survey.

Kind regards

Rockets Reading Group

1. Do you separate rubbish in your household?
2. Which items do you separate?
3. Does your kitchen have a waste disposal unit?
4. Do you have a compost bin?
5. What are the benefits of recycling?
6. What makes recycling in the home difficult?

We are developing a summary statement using the results of this survey. We will send this home when it is completed.

Thank you for your time.

11 Plus, minus, interesting chart (PMI chart)

Students record their thoughts about the text or issues raised in the text under the headings as shown. Use the photocopy master PM 3 on page 76.

PMI chart for: recycling   Your name: Ari

PLUS	MINUS	INTERESTING
• Doesn't waste resources • Feeds animals on farms, e.g. pigs and hens	• Inconvenient to separate rubbish • Time consuming	• In the past people recycled as a matter of necessity

PMI chart idea from *Teaching Thinking* by Edward de Bono

12 Cause and effect chart

Students identify the *cause* (why something happened) and its *effect* (what happened). This concept can be developed in a number of ways. Write a set of cards with causes written on some cards and their effects on others and have the students match the cards. Students could also identify which part of a sentence was the cause and which part the effect by underlining the cause. For example, <u>Harry got tired and hungry</u> so he decided to go home. A cause and effect flow chart as illustrated works well for both narrative and factual text and can be generic or text specific.

Cause and effect charts

Cause: Harry hated having a bath
Effect: He buried his scrubbing brush and ran away from home.

↓

Cause: Harry played near some men mending the street.
Effect: He got very dirty.

↓

Cause: Harry got extremely dirty.
Effect: He changed from being a white dog with black spots to a black dog with white spots.

↓

Cause: Harry got tired and hungry.
Effect: He decided to go home.

↓

Cause: Harry's family didn't recognise him.
Effect: He performed all his old tricks.

↓

Cause: Harry found his scrubbing brush and ran to the bath.
Effect: The children gave Harry a bath.

↓

Cause: The water cleaned away all the black dirt from Harry's coat.
Effect: The family discovered it was Harry after all.

Based on *Harry the Dirty Dog* by Gene Zion

Your ideas

Chapter 2

Focusing on words

Other responses that focus on words are:

- Quotes
- Character rating chart
- Sequencing text
- Character web
- Checklist
- Y chart
- Grid organiser

1 Predict and check chart

During the reading of unseen text, students identify vocabulary of which they are unsure. Using the context of the story and their prior knowledge, they make an attempt to predict the meaning of the word. Finally they check the dictionary for the 'expert' definition. Use the photocopy master PM 4 on page 77.

This idea can also be used for students' own questions relating to the text. Students ask questions, make predictions, then use reference material to locate correct information.

Predict and check chart   Your name: Sara

Title and author	Word	Page	Your definition	Expert definition
Plants that Store Water by Gillian Shannon	desert	7	A dry place where cactus grow	A barren, uninhabited, often sandy region
	cactus	7	A plant that is sharp and prickly	A fleshy plant, often with prickles, from a dry hot climate
	succulents	9	A plant that can hold water	A plant that has thick fleshy leaves or stems

Questions	What I think	What I found out	Where I found the information
What plants grow in Australian deserts?			
What is the hottest temperature ever recorded in an Australian desert?			

Based on *Plants that Store Water* by Gillian Shannon

2 Predict the words

This is a quick starter activity to assist students to focus on vocabulary and orientate them to the text they are about to read. For independent reading: students read the title and jot down a list of about five or six words they predict will be in the text. If the word does appear in the text they tick it off on their list. This could also be done orally with the teacher at the beginning of a small group reading session. The teacher records the students' responses and the list is reviewed briefly at the end of the reading session.

Learning to be a knight
Words I predict will be in the story

- horse
- sowrd.
- midevial
- armour
- castle
- Helmets
- Boots

3 Word search

Students plot words from the story onto a grid horizontally, vertically and diagonally. They then add random letters to fill the grid. Use the photocopy master PM 5 on page 78. Students swap grids with a partner who has to locate the hidden words. A variation on this could be to have a particular focus, for example, words that describe a particular character, and the partner must guess who the character is.

Word search for The Gruffalo

Author: Julia Donaldson

B	R	G	U	L	L	I	B	L	E	C	D
S	L	F	G	B	C	R	E	T	B	K	M
A	H	A	I	R	Y	G	F	U	A	O	E
V	K	H	C	I	J	K	Y	S	Z	R	P
P	R	I	C	K	L	E	S	K	A	S	U
V	A	B	A	L	T	B	W	S	X	B	Q
F	E	H	U	G	E	O	R	A	N	G	E
H	W	T	M	H	I	J	N	V	W	R	Y
J	U	A	S	T	R	T	U	G	P	L	E
W	N	O	R	P	Q	R	O	T	U	V	S
B	V	E	U	T	A	E	H	G	D	E	C
K	N	O	B	B	L	Y	K	N	E	E	S

Created by: **Jack**

Completed by: **Dylan**

Based on *The Gruffalo* by Julia Donaldson

4 Cloze activities

STUDENT OUTCOMES
- Developing comprehension through in-depth reading
- Providing opportunities to focus on specific areas of student need

Traditionally, cloze activities have been used after reading to check comprehension. Words or punctuation are deleted from a sentence or passage of text. Students fill in the gaps to make the sentence or passage make sense. Cloze activities are useful to target the specific needs of students, such as use of correct tense or forms of punctuation. Random cloze, where random words are deleted, can be used as an introduction to unseen text. Sets of generic cloze activities could be prepared by the teacher and stored in resealable plastic bags. Each set could contain photocopies of the cloze activity and an overhead transparency of the correct text.

Example one

Targeted cloze: to focus on tense (student crosses out incorrect answers)

Goldilocks (eat, eating, ate) Baby Bear's porridge.
The bears (come, coming, came) home from their walk in the forest.
Baby Bear found Goldilocks (sleep, sleeping, slept) in his bed.

Example two

Random cloze: to use as an introduction to unseen text (student fills in missing words)

Shark Skin: random cloze

Whereas most fish _____ large scales, a shark's skin is covered in microscopic tooth-like scales called denticles. If you were to _____ the skin one way it would be smooth like the fur of a cat. Brush the skin the other way and it would be _____ like sandpaper. Like the _____ of the shark, the denticles are pointed, covered with enamel and contain a nerve. Denticles can be shed and _____ again.

Shark Skin: original text
Whereas most fish have large scales, a shark's skin is covered in microscopic tooth-like scales called denticles. If you were to brush the skin one way it would be smooth like the fur of a cat. Brush the skin the other way and it would be rough like sandpaper. Like the teeth of the shark, the denticles are pointed, covered with enamel and contain a nerve. Denticles can be shed and grown again.

5 Best word

STUDENT OUTCOMES
- Building vocabulary knowledge
- Learning to justify choice of word with an appropriate reason

Each student is given a sticky note. During independent reading of the text, the student chooses a word he or she didn't know the meaning of, liked the sound of, recognised a root word in, or appealed to him or her for a particular reason. The student then records the word on the sticky note. When the students meet with the teacher for their reading session, each student puts his or her sticky note on a chart and briefly tells the group why he or she chose that word and, if necessary, explains the meaning. This is a quick starter activity that should take no longer than five minutes.

pharmacopoeia

6 Word cline

STUDENT OUTCOMES
- **Extending and enriching vocabulary**
- **Developing co-operative learning skills**

Clines focus on the intensity of meanings of words. Words can be written on cards or sticky notes. Students place them on the cline (slope) according to their strength of meaning. This may be done independently, then discussed with a partner or small group to come to a consensus.

The Descriptive words chart photocopy master (PM 19, page 94), or a Thesaurus would assist students to create their own word clines.

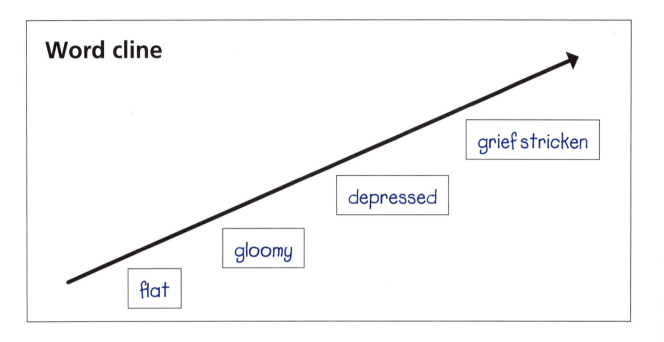

Word cline

grief stricken

depressed

gloomy

flat

7 Bingo game

STUDENT OUTCOMES
- **Building rapid recognition of basic words**
- **Developing listening skills**

This activity is useful for learning basic words. Make a set of bingo boards containing eight to twelve words. Each board has a slightly different set of words. Make a master board that includes all the words used on all the boards. Each member of the group has a bingo card, and the teacher or a capable student is the caller. The caller says a word from the master list and if students have that word on their board they cover it up with a counter. The winner is the person who covers his or her bingo board first. To indicate that his or her board is covered, the student calls out 'bingo'. The student calls out each of the words on their board and the caller checks it on the master list.

It is beneficial to play this game over a number of consecutive sessions.

because	know	always	people
now	friend	where	thought
should	going	only	when

8 Word match

This is a pre-reading activity to introduce new vocabulary in a text. The teacher selects vocabulary that may be challenging for the students. Words and their meanings are listed in two columns so the word does not match the meaning. Students must match the word with the correct meaning by drawing a line from the word to its meaning.

Word match

Draw a line to match the word with its meaning

dowry	a race on foot of 42.195 kilometres
delirious	to give or assume new vitality
hallucinations	to prevent
revive	a person who engages in an activity for no monetary gain
hinder	the alleged perception of an object when no object is present
marathon	wildly excited, especially with joy or enthusiasm
amateur	money or property brought by a woman to her husband at marriage

Based on *The First Olympic Marathon* by Douglas Carion

9 Split sentences

The teacher writes sentences from the text onto strips of card, then splits them by cutting it in two. All the strips are randomly laid upside down. Students take a turn at picking up two strips and reading them to see if they match. If the two strips match they can keep them, if not, they must put them back. The student with the most completed sentences wins. By splitting the sentence at an appropriate point, this activity can be used to highlight particular teaching points such as quotation marks and commas.

Split sentences

The giant hummingbird lives in the

mountains, where its size helps it cope with the cold.

All hummingbirds have tubed-shaped beaks

found only in North and South America.

is nearly as long as its body.

The sword-billed hummingbird's beak

beat more than 70 times a minute.

Ruby throated hummingbirds' wings

There are about 340 species of hummingbirds,

and lap up their food with their tongues.

10 Sequencing text and/or pictures

STUDENT OUTCOMES
- Developing ability to monitor own comprehension
- Identifying correct sequence

Sequencing the text can be done on many levels, from sequencing the letters in one word to the words in a sentence, to sequencing a passage of text.

Pictures can also be sequenced and the story retold orally or in written form. Prepared text can be matched to the pictures, or students could write their own. Alternatively they could sequence strips of the text and draw pictures to match.

b a n a n a

I | can | make | a | banana | smoothie

Wash and dry your hands thoroughly.	You will need some milk, yoghurt and a banana.	Measure out 2 table-spoons of yoghurt and 1 cup of milk.	Pour the yoghurt and the milk into the blender.
Peel the banana and cut it into pieces.	Put the cut-up banana in the blender with the milk and yoghurt.	Turn the blender on to high and blend until smooth.	Pour the banana smoothie into a glass and enjoy!

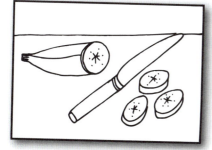  

Your ideas

Chapter 3

Exploring characters, setting and plot

Other responses that include exploring characters, setting and plot are:

- Board game
- Caption mural
- Drawing for comprehension
- Story cube
- Narrative outline
- Dialogue journal
- Facts and opinions
- Who am I?
- Prop box
- 'Pick a card' activity
- Timeline
- Reward poster
- Advertisement
- Television or radio news item
- Book review
- Book assignments
- Dialogue journal
- Conversations
- Wall story
- Cause and effect chart
- Model making
- Puppet making
- Mask making
- Overhead projector play
- Which came first?
- Read and retell

1 Diorama

A diorama is a three-dimensional snapshot of a part of a story. Students create their own visual image of the setting and characters. While dioramas are more commonly used with narrative text, they can also be used to illustrate factual text, for example, an animal habitat or a model of a planet. Don't forget to add a piece of card at the bottom of the diorama for the student to write a title, his or her name, and an explanation of what the diorama is about.

Shoebox diorama

Have the students paint or dye the interior of the box, then work on more detailed parts like figure making while the paint is drying. Use coloured pencils or marker pens for smaller details.

Modelling clay or plasticine can be used to make figures or animals. Items can be hung from the top of the box with nylon thread. Realia such as sand, twigs, moss, fabric for wallpaper, and so on can be added for effect if appropriate. Cellophane helps creates the illusion of water and cotton wool can be used for clouds.

Note: factory shoe shops are a good source of bulk shoeboxes.

AMOS AND BORIS
William Steig

Based on *Amos and Boris* by William Steig

Triangle diorama

Triangle dioramas provide a quick way of making a background structure for a diorama. Use light card and follow directions as shown. Dioramas can sit on a shelf or be stapled or taped to a wall.

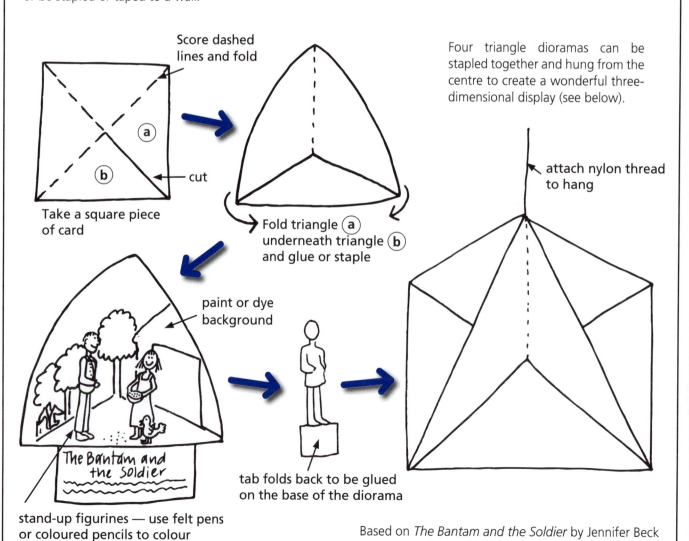

Score dashed lines and fold

(a)
(b) — cut

Take a square piece of card

Fold triangle (a) underneath triangle (b) and glue or staple

paint or dye background

The Bantam and the Soldier

stand-up figurines — use felt pens or coloured pencils to colour

tab folds back to be glued on the base of the diorama

Four triangle dioramas can be stapled together and hung from the centre to create a wonderful three-dimensional display (see below).

attach nylon thread to hang

Based on *The Bantam and the Soldier* by Jennifer Beck

2 Venn diagram

Venn diagrams compare two characters. Use the photocopy master PM 6 on page 79. On the two outer sides of the circles the children write the characteristics of each of the two characters. In the overlapping section they write the characteristics that are common to both characters. As characters may change during the course of the story, it is necessary to specify which part of the story the Venn diagram illustrates. Venn diagrams can also be used to compare two characters from two different stories, or the student could compare himself or herself to a particular character. Venn diagrams also provide a planning structure for comparative writing.

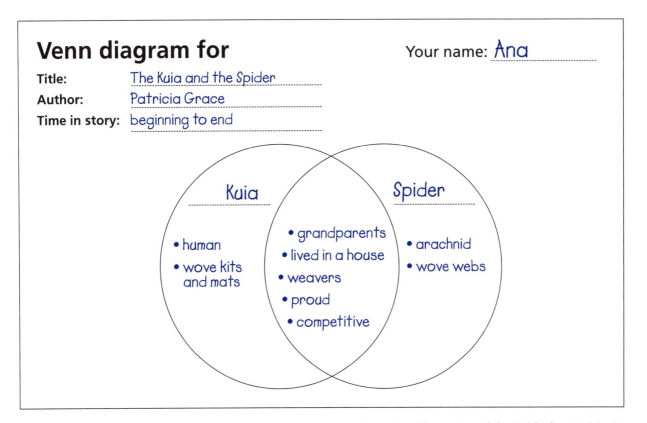

Venn diagram for　　　　　　Your name: Ana

Title: The Kuia and the Spider
Author: Patricia Grace
Time in story: beginning to end

Kuia
- human
- wove kits and mats

- grandparents
- lived in a house
- weavers
- proud
- competitive

Spider
- arachnid
- wove webs

Based on *The Kuia and the Spider* by Patricia Grace

3 Business card

Students design a business card for a character in the text. If possible have the students look at a selection of business cards and discuss their language and visual features. It may be easier for students to design the card on a larger piece of paper such as A5 then reduce it on a photocopier. This response can be appropriate for both narrative and factual text.

No dastardly deed too small!

Mr A Wolf
General Nuisance
4 Forrest Drive
Storylandville

Phone 878 5601
Fax 878 5602
Wolf line 025 6841
www.hireavillain.com

4 Sociogram

Sociograms analyse the relationships between characters in a story. This can be introduced on a simple level where students identify family relationships such as mother, father, grandfather, cousin, and so on. More complex relationships can be developed as the student becomes familiar with the response. Circles are drawn to represent characters, with the main character placed in the middle. Arrows are drawn between characters, showing the direction of the relationship, and brief statements written to describe the nature of the relationship. Teachers can direct the students to focus their sociogram on any number of areas, such as stated and inferred feelings.

Sociogram for

Your name: Rowan

Title The Tale of Peter Rabbit
Author Beatrix Potter
Time in story beginning to end

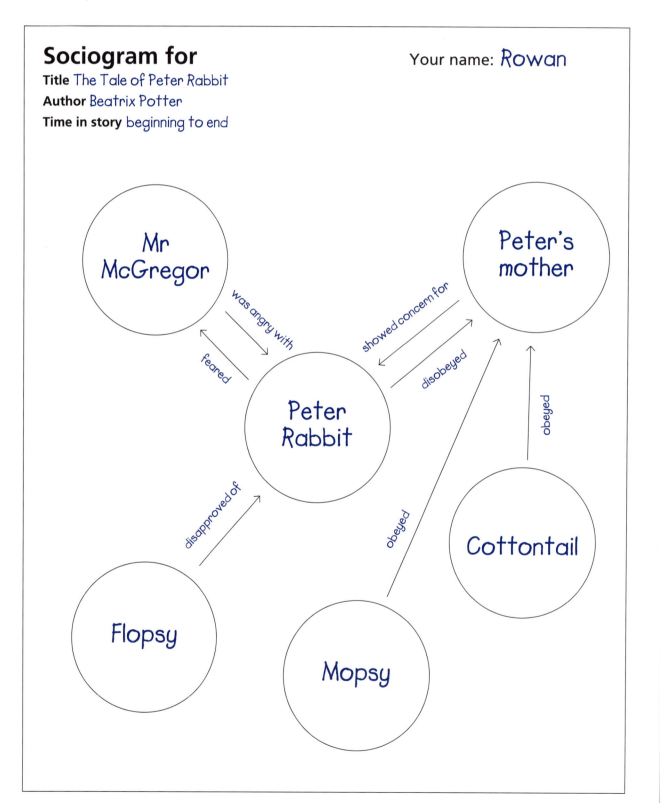

Based on *The Tale of Peter Rabbit* by Beatrix Potter

5 Character costumes

Newspaper and masking tape costume

Students work in pairs to create a costume. Each pair is given newspaper and masking tape. Attach long strips of masking tape to the side of a table or desk beside each pair so students can cut shorter lengths themselves. Give the class a time limit of approximately 20 minutes. At the end of the making session, have a character parade where one partner models the costume and the other partner explains the features of the costume. As this activity can be noisy it may be more appropriate as a whole class activity in response to a read aloud. The first time the students try this activity they could choose a character from a story they are already familiar with, such as a fairytale, and have the rest of the class guess who they are.

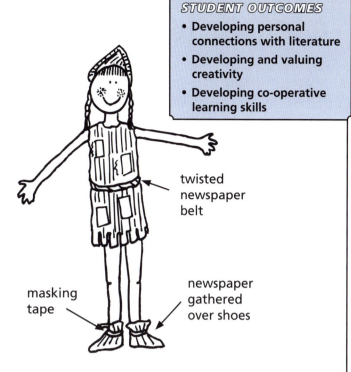

twisted newspaper belt

masking tape

newspaper gathered over shoes

Peg doll character

Students dress their wooden peg as a character. Provide yarn, sheepskin, string or craft paper for hair and scraps of fabric and leather for clothing. Pipe cleaners can be used for arms. Having an extra adult and a hot glue gun is helpful in this activity.

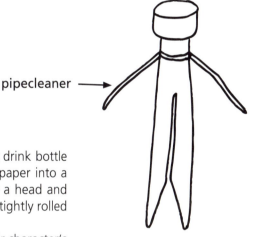

pipecleaner

Bottle person

Students create a character out of a plastic bottle. Use a small plastic drink bottle and fill it with rice or sand to weigh it down. Crush a piece of newspaper into a ball, cover with some white paper, draw together and tape to make a head and neck. Cut holes in the side of the bottle and thread through a piece of tightly rolled newspaper to make arms. Dress in clothes made from paper or fabric.

Encourage the students to find quotes from the story that describe their character's appearance.

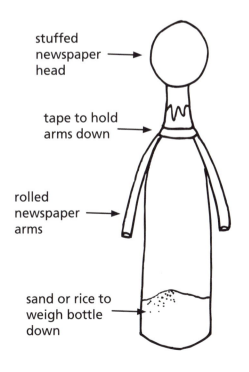

stuffed newspaper head

tape to hold arms down

rolled newspaper arms

sand or rice to weigh bottle down

6 Character portrait

Pencil drawings are an appropriate medium for this activity as they take a minimal amount of teacher preparation and enable the child to show a lot of detail. Remember pencil drawing is an intimate form of drawing, so keep the size of the paper small. A5 or smaller is an appropriate size. Ask the students to use their pencil to show you as many different things about the character as they can. A web structure could be used to plan the portrait using quotes from the story that describe the character's appearance.

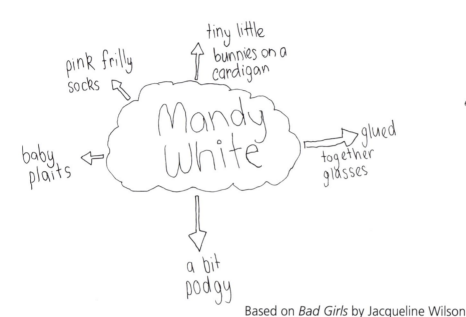

Based on *Bad Girls* by Jacqueline Wilson

7 Character diary

Student takes on the role of a character and writes a diary for that character over a specified period of time. The timespan for the diary entry may be for a day or longer, depending on the amount of action taking place.

Norvin's diary

23 January
I am really getting annoyed at all those tourists swimming at the cove. At the beginning of summer I could swim the whole way across the bay and not bump into a single person. Today was hopeless. I wish those blasted tourists would all go back to where they came from so I could have the beach to myself again. The only good thing about the day was when Mum made doughnuts for pudding.

24 January
What a brilliant day!
I lay awake in bed last night trying to think of a plan to get the beach back to myself again, and came up with a ripper!
I borrowed some of Dad's tools and an old sheet of plastic I found in the garage and made this really cool fake dorsal fin. It looks like a real shark one! I went round the headland out of sight of the swimmers, strapped it on and swam across the bay. It was amazing! I couldn't believe how petrified people were. Mrs Scorpio from the cake shop raced out of the water – I have never seen her move so fast!
The really good thing is that I have the beach all to myself again!

Based on *The Great White Man-Eating Shark* by Margaret Mahy

8 The hot seat: character interview

One student takes on the role of a particular character and is put in the 'hot seat'. The character in the 'hot seat' could wear a hat or an item of clothing to suggest the character being portrayed. Younger students could wear a sign around their neck with the character's name on it. The other members of the group ask the 'character' pre-prepared questions. Depending on the text, the questions may be general or focused on a specific time or event.

It may be helpful to model question stems such as:

> In the story you said …
> Why did you …?
> How did you feel when …?
> If you were in that situation again would you …?
> What is your opinion about …?

Students could also play 'mystery hot seat' where they ask questions to guess who the character in the 'hot seat' is.

9 Character grid organiser

This grid organiser is used to gather information under prescribed headings. Use the photocopy master PM 7 on page 80. The Descriptive words chart photocopy master (PM 19, page 94) would be a helpful support.

The information could be used to write an individual character study or to compare two or more characters from the same or a different book. Students could also compare a character to themselves.

Character grid organiser for: Crash! The story of Poddy

Character	Physical appearance	Personal characteristics
Poddy (Patrick)	short round black hair Downs Syndrome	perplexed insecure dependent heroic
Jack	tall athletic slim blondish hair	sulky earnest proud arrogant dominant tolerant

Based on *Crash! The story of Poddy* by William Taylor

10 Ideas for character writing responses

- Write an epilogue for a character. What will your character be doing in one month? one year? five years?

EPILOGUE FOR DANNY

1 months time

Danny will be playing baseball in the Hazellwood junior team.

1 years time

Danny and his dad will own a vegetarian store across the road from their caravan.

5 years time

Danny will start to babysit Mrs Clipstones baby boy.

Based on *Danny, the Champion of the World* by Roald Dahl

Epilogue For Fudge

In one month's time

He will still stay on the toilet to irritate Peter

In five year's time

He will stop annoying his big brother.

In ten year's time

He will play with tootsie

In twenty years time

He will own Washington and call it Fudgeington

Based on *Fudge-a-mania* by Judy Blume

- Write a letter to a character expressing an opinion.

Dear Mr Hazell,
You are a disgrace to man kind. Please take notice that pheasants are an endangered species so you shouldn't be killing them. If you do it again we will arrest you. Thank you for taking the time to read this letter.

Signed Seargent E. Samways.

Based on *Danny, the Champion of the World* by Roald Dahl

- Write about a time you felt the same way as one of the characters in the book or had a similar experience.

Once my grandad got my cousin a whole set of books. My cousin already had one of the books from the set so my brother blurted out: "I think he already has one of 'those'." I was really embarrassed. Luckily nobody heard.

This is like the time Fudge brings out an old picture dictionary, when Peter just recieves a new one!

Based on *Superfudge* by Judy Blume

- Write about the character you would most want to meet and why.

I would like to meet fudge from Superfudge
I would like to meet Fudge because he is a funny character He does things like sticking stamps on his sister and eating flowers. He is cheeky like he answers his mum back. And he likes to stay with his big brother Peter
Fudge would be a funny person to meet!!!!!!!!

Emma

Based on *Superfudge* by Judy Blume

- Write a letter to the character of your choice. Have a friend reply to your letter as that character.
- Retell the story in the role of different character, for example, from the giant's point of view in *Jack and the Beanstalk*.

11 Excitement chart

An excitement chart plots the level of action over the course of a short passage, a chapter, or an entire book, depending on the amount of action taking place. It could also focus on how a particular character is feeling as the action in the story unfolds. The Descriptive words chart photocopy master (PM 19, page 94) could assist students to do this. Students could plan the timeline part of the excitement chart co-operatively and then focus on a different character each, so comparisons could be made from different points of view.

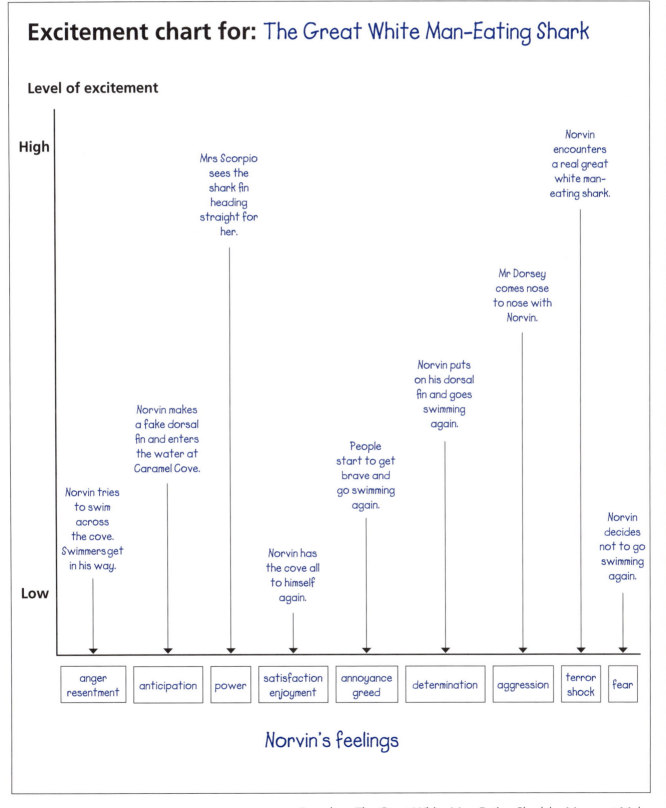

Excitement chart for: The Great White Man-Eating Shark

Level of excitement

High

Mrs Scorpio sees the shark fin heading straight for her.

Norvin encounters a real great white man-eating shark.

Mr Dorsey comes nose to nose with Norvin.

Norvin puts on his dorsal fin and goes swimming again.

Norvin makes a fake dorsal fin and enters the water at Caramel Cove.

People start to get brave and go swimming again.

Norvin tries to swim across the cove. Swimmers get in his way.

Norvin has the cove all to himself again.

Norvin decides not to go swimming again.

Low

anger resentment	anticipation	power	satisfaction enjoyment	annoyance greed	determination	aggression	terror shock	fear

Norvin's feelings

Based on *The Great White Man-Eating Shark* by Margaret Mahy

12 Character web

Students choose a character from the story and prepare a web of words appropriate to that character. Each word or phrase must be followed by a statement that supports his or her thinking. Use the photocopy master PM 8 on page 81. Thesauri, dictionaries or the Descriptive words chart photocopy master (PM 19, page 94) could be used to extend vocabulary. This web could also be used as a planning structure to write a character description.

Character web

Your name: Samantha

Title: The Great White Man-Eating Shark

Author: Margaret Mahy

Illustrator: Jonathan Allen

Character: Norvin

Time in story: beginning to end

creative

he designed and constructed a fake dorsal fin

cross and resentful

because he wanted the beach all to himself

Norvin

unkind

he terrorised people intentionally

determined

when swimmers went back into the water after the first shark scare, Norvin put on his fake dorsal fin again and swam across the bay to ensure he could have the beach to himself

proud

of his swimming ability – he was able to shoot through the water like a silver arrow

Based on *The Great White Man-Eating Shark* by Margaret Mahy

13 Story map

STUDENT OUTCOMES
- Developing comprehension through in-depth reading
- Developing concepts of scale and overview

A story map is a bird's-eye view of the setting in which a story takes place. Story maps can illustrate relatively small areas such as a rabbit's burrow or have much wider overviews such as for stories that move across several countries. Story maps also provide a structure for students to retell the story. Many published texts include examples that would be useful illustrations for students. *Winnie the Pooh* by A.A. Milne contains a story map, as does *The Hobbit* by J.R.R. Tolkien.

Story map for: Little Red Riding Hood

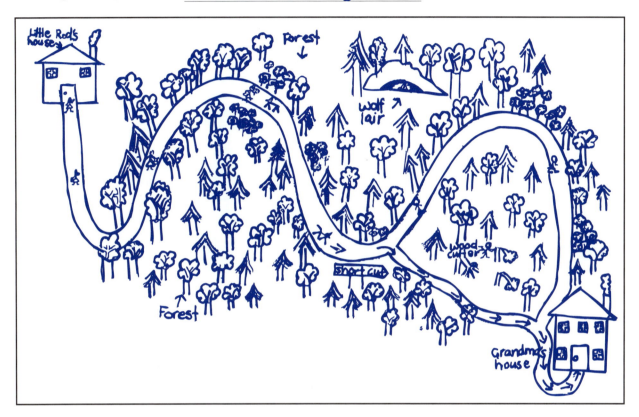

14 Quotes

STUDENT OUTCOMES
- Learning to inference
- Developing scanning skills

Teacher selects one or more quotes from the text. Students clarify their meaning.

Alternatively, students find a quote that typifies a particular character and justify their choice.

Both these ideas would work well as written responses or small group discussion sessions.

Quotes are also useful to support visual responses such as dioramas or character portraits. Have the students find three quotes that describe the setting or the character's appearance.

> 'That's a lovely idea, it would really cheer Grandma up to get a bunch of fresh bluebells.'

This quote is from page 4 in the story when the wolf lures Little Red Riding Hood into the forest to look for bluebells for her grandmother. I think it shows how naive she was. Little Red didn't realise the wolf's intentions even though her mother had warned her to be careful.

15 Character rating chart

STUDENT OUTCOMES
- **Developing comprehension through in-depth reading**
- **Developing analysis skills**

Students rate characters against a set of adjectives. The teacher or students could generate the adjectives. Use the photocopy master PM 9 on page 82. The Descriptive words chart photocopy master (PM 19, page 94) would be helpful. Students also justify their rating by writing a sentence to support their thinking.

Character rating chart

Story: Jim and the Beanstalk

Author: Raymond Briggs

Time in story: beginning

Your name: Sean

Rating key: ✗ means not at all like the adjective described
✔ means a little like the adjective described
✔✔ means quite like the adjective described
✔✔✔ means very much like the adjective described

Adjective	Character				Justification
	Jim	Giant			
frightening	✗	✔✔✔			The giant was very frightening at the beginning because he was so huge and wasn't very friendly.
contented	✔✔	✗			Jim seemed quite contented but the giant wasn't because he had lost his hair and his teeth and couldn't see very well.
generous	✔✔✔	✗			Jim was very generous to the giant because he helped him.
courageous	✔✔✔	✗			Jim was very courageous to keep helping the giant when he wasn't sure if the giant would eat him.

Based on *Jim and the Beanstalk* by Raymond Briggs

16 Character book assignment

STUDENT OUTCOMES
• Encouraging student independence
• Providing opportunities for student choice, which increases motivation

Students choose a character and complete various activities focusing on that character. Use the photocopy master PM 10 on page 83.

Character book assignment

Fill in the 'pizza'!

Find a song that reflects your character's personality.

Think of an occasion in the book when you would have acted differently from your character. Write about what happened and what you would have done.

Design a business card for your character.

Think of a fun name for your character. Explain why you have chosen it.

Find a quote in your book that typifies your character. Explain why.

Write a diary for a day in the life of your character.

Write a paragraph telling what your character will be doing in five years' time.

Develop a character web for your character.

I agree to complete ___4___ of the above activities. The character I have chosen to focus on is _____Norvin_____ from the story _____The Great White Man-Eating Shark_____ .

I agree to have my character contract completed by _____25 August_____ .

Signed   Student: _____Jack Smith_____

Teacher: _____Mrs Jones_____

Date: _____11 August_____

Colour in each 'pizza' segment when you have completed the task.

Based on *The Great White Man-Eating Shark* by Margaret Mahy

Your ideas

Chapter 4

Creating visual responses

Other responses that include visual aspects are:

- Wall story
- Circular story
- Timeline
- Flow chart
- Storyboard
- Sequencing pictures
- Diorama
- Business card
- Character costumes
- Character portrait
- Story map
- Postcard
- Dust jacket
- Caption mural
- Overhead projector play
- Barrier games
- Prop box

1 Bookmark

Students design a bookmark to promote one or more books by a particular author.

Use light-coloured card and laminate or cover with clear contact paper. Punch a hole at the bottom and tie on some coloured ribbon or string.

Students will love to use their special bookmark at silent reading time!

2 Model making

Students design a three-dimensional model appropriate to the text. For example, using cardboard and masking tape, the students could construct a shark fin belt as worn by Norvin in the *The Great White Man-Eating Shark* by Margaret Mahy. Alternatively, students could invent a machine that could do a particular job. This could be a quick drawing or could be developed into a scale model. An overhead transparency drawing is a good way for students to share their model or machine plan with their classmates.

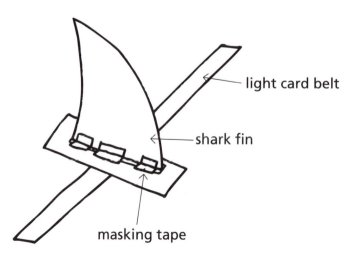

light card belt

shark fin

masking tape

3 Brochure

Students create a brochure or pamphlet to advertise a place or event appropriate to the text.

As this is a challenging and time-consuming task it may work better to have pairs of students working on components of the brochure. These could then be collated.

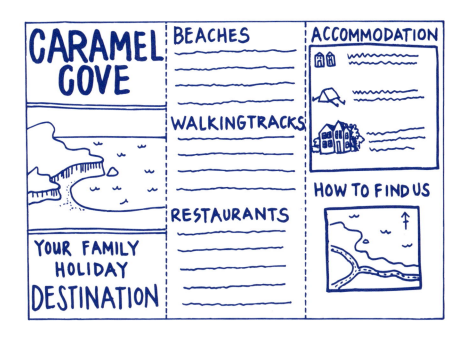

Based on *The Great White Man-Eating Shark* by Margaret Mahy

4 Author or illustrator poster

Students design a poster to encourage others to read one of their favourite authors' or illustrators' work. Posters could be displayed in the school or public library.

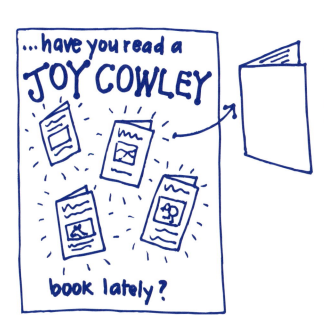

Each 'book' could open up and contain a blurb about the story inside.

5 Reward poster

Students create a reward poster for a missing character or 'baddie' in the text. Students could further develop their description into a piece of writing or read it aloud and have other students guess which character they are describing.

WANTED!

To read more about Kim, take a look at BAD GIRLS by J.Wilson

Kim Matthews

Friends =

– For terrorizing Mandy White.

– Teasing Arthur King.

– Being smart to Mrs. Stanley.

– Not being loyal to her friends.

REWARD = £10,000.5*

Features =
– Black hair   – Walks by self
– Very tall

*5¢ extra because you deserve to share this money with a friend.

Based on *Bad Girls* by Jacqueline Wilson

6 Stamp

This response is appropriate for both narrative and factual texts. Students view and discuss the visual language features of stamps, then design their own stamp appropriate to the text read. Use the photocopy master PM 11 on page 84.

Factual text example: Students design a stamp depicting a New Zealand mushroom after reading an article on fungi of New Zealand.

Narrative text example: Students design a stamp appropriate for Caramel Cove in *The Great White Man-Eating Shark* by Margaret Mahy.

This activity could just be a quick pencil sketch or could be taken to a high level of publication.

7 Board game

Students design a board game around the theme of a story. Actual events from the story may be included or the game may be just based on the story. Use the photocopy master PM 12 on page 85, enlarge it to A3 size and laminate or glue to card. Remember to make this an authentic activity by providing counters and dice so the game can be played. Store in resealable plastic bags to be used as an independent reading activity. The addition of 'Good Luck' and 'Bad Luck' cards can add to the fun. When players land on a square that has 'Good Luck' written on it, they pick up a card that contains good fortune such as 'You slay the dragon — go on 5 spaces'. 'Bad Luck' cards may require you to go back spaces or miss a turn. Encourage the students to use events in the story as a basis for writing these cards.

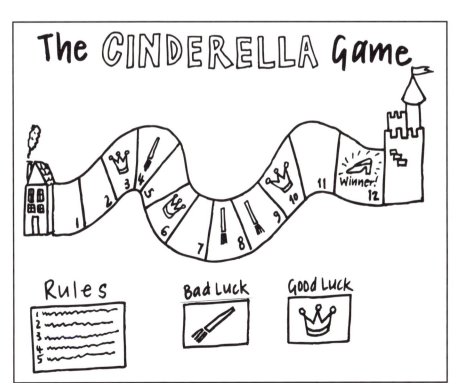

8 Ticket

STUDENT OUTCOMES
- Extending ideas beyond the text
- Combining written and visual features to create a ticket

Stories often involve a journey or an event. Chris van Allsburg's Christmas story, *The Polar Express,* is a wonderful example of this. Discuss the language features of tickets; some tickets have minimal information whereas others such as airline tickets have very detailed information. A collection of tickets would help to demonstrate this. Students design a ticket appropriate to a journey or event in the text.

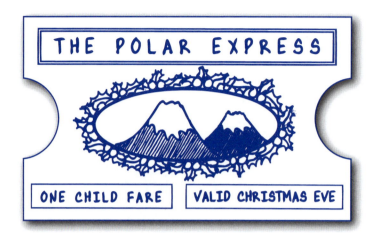

Based on *The Polar Express* by Chris van Allsburg

9 Caption mural

STUDENT OUTCOMES
- Providing demonstrations of the way language works
- Developing personal connections with literature

Students represent a scene from the text or the whole story on a large sheet of paper. Some students paint or dye the background while others create characters that can be glued on later. The captions could retell the original story, be an innovation on the text or be responses from the students about the text.

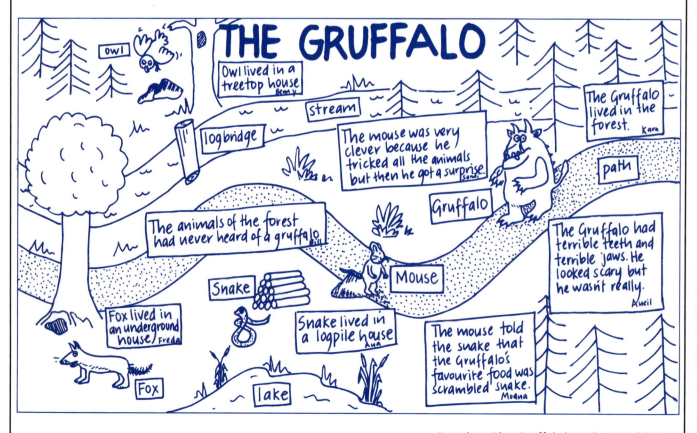

Based on *The Gruffalo* by Julie Donaldson

10 Catalogue

Students design a catalogue to advertise a set of items appropriate to the text. Students could design a catalogue individually, with a buddy or in a small group. Have samples of catalogues available and discuss the written and visual features common to catalogues.

Each student or group of students responsible for a catalogue could then create a 'sales pitch' to convince others to buy their products.

11 Cross-section and cut-away diagrams

A cross-section is an analytical diagram that takes a slice through the centre of an object to reveal the core. A cut-away diagram takes a look at an object layer by layer in a three-dimensional way.

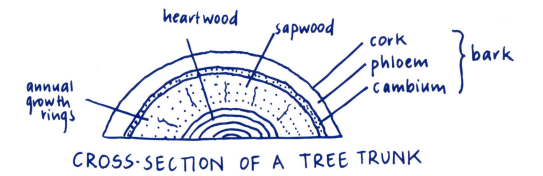

CROSS-SECTION OF A TREE TRUNK

12 Puppet making

A variety of puppets can be designed and made from simple materials. When completed, store the puppets and the play scripts in a resealable plastic bag to create an independent reading activity. Puppets could also be added to a prop box (see page 65).

sock puppet

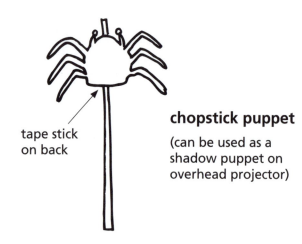

chopstick puppet

(can be used as a shadow puppet on overhead projector)

finger puppet 1

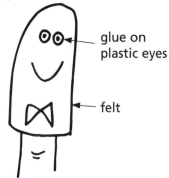

finger puppet 2

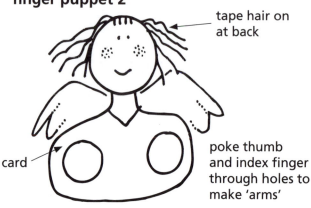

13 Mask making

Masks can be used as minimal costumes for plays or Readers Theatre scripts. Some ideas for making hair are wool (yarn and sheepskin), crepe paper, leather, curled pipe cleaners, string, shredded paper, cellophane or tissue.

STUDENT OUTCOMES
- Providing a springboard for oral language
- Developing creativity and opportunities for individual response

paper bag

paper plate

icecream container lid or card

14 Drawing for comprehension

STUDENT OUTCOMES
- Clarifying thinking
- Transferring written information into a visual format to aid comprehension

Students sketch a part of the text to help clarify their understanding. For example the teacher may ask the students to do a quick sketch to show a setting such as the layout of a room or the life cycle of an animal as described in the text. Students should be encouraged to include as much detail as they can to demonstrate their understanding. Drawing can be done during an instructional reading session, or after the reading.

Another idea, suitable for a book assignment, is to have the students choose a place or setting in a novel they have read. They use the description in the book to draw a realistic 'photo' of that place. Students then paste descriptive quotes copied from the book under their 'photo'.

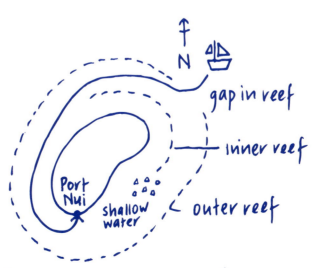
Passage of the 'Raider'

15 Greeting card or certificate

Design a card, invitation or certificate appropriate to the text. Some ideas for cards could be birthday, get well, anniversary, congratulations, sympathy, new home or bon voyage. Certificates could be designed to acknowledge characters' achievements such as overcoming a personal obstacle or winning a race.

Based on *Danny, the Champion of the World* by Roald Dahl

16 Story cube

Students construct a cube using the template and instructions given on the photocopy master PM 13 on page 86. The master may be photocopied onto light card or glued onto cardboard. Enlarge the photocopy master to A3 size to make larger cubes. Students complete the story cube as indicated on the instructions. Story cubes can be hung using nylon thread to make a mobile.

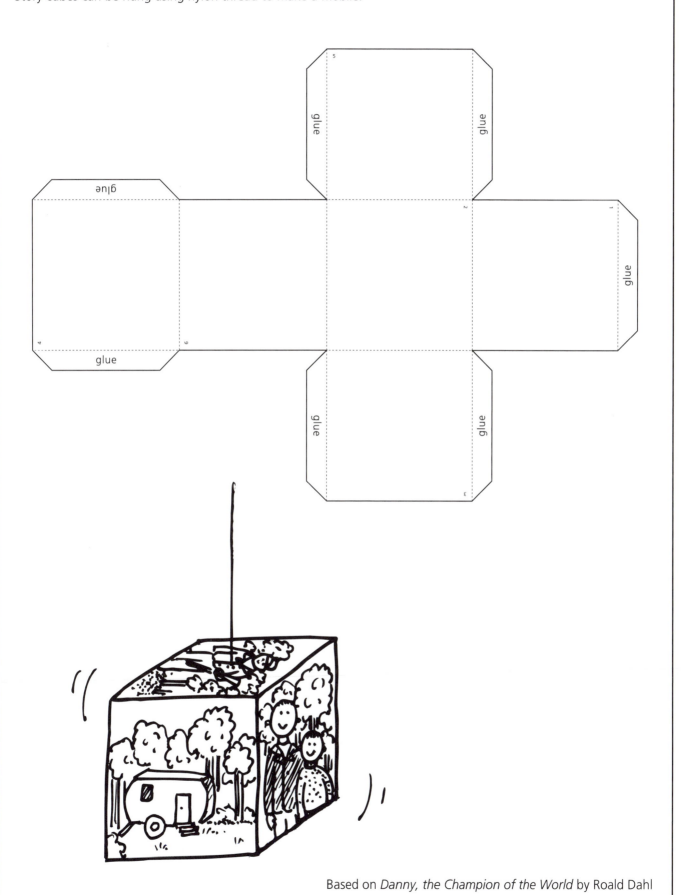

Based on *Danny, the Champion of the World* by Roald Dahl

Your ideas

Chapter 5

Engaging in writing

Other responses that include writing are:

- Storyboard
- Flowchart
- Character diary
- Character writing responses
- Quotes
- Read and retell
- Timeline
- Who am I?
- Brochure
- Character web
- Character book assignment
- Circular story
- Cause and effect chart
- Readers Theatre
- Conversations
- Survey
- Quotes
- Caption mural
- Conversations

1 Advertisement

Students create an advertisement for something appropriate to the book they have read. For example, after reading *The Polar Express* by Chris van Allsburg, they could create a job vacancy advertisement for chefs to work on the Polar Express. Advertisements could also be created for products or services and presented in oral, visual or written form.

JOB VACANCY

CHEFS FOR POLAR EXPRESS

Two chefs are required for night of 24 December only.

Duties include preparation and serving of sweets and hot cocoa. Must enjoy working with children. Pay rates on enquiry.

Please contact F. Christmas on 0800northpole or email f.christmas@northpole.com

2 Radio or television news item

Students put themselves in a neutral position and report on an event in the style of a news reporter. Items could be read orally to a group or the class in a 'news reading' style.

SHARK SCARE A HOAX

Caramel Cove residents and holiday makers have recently been plagued by sightings of a great white man-eating shark. It was revealed today that the 'shark' was a local boy wearing a dorsal fin made out of plastic. Mr Dorsey, a local plumber who had himself left the water in previous days after sightings of the shark, said he was most disappointed by the actions of the boy but was pleased the beach was safe to swim in again.

Based on *The Great White Man-Eating Shark* by Margaret Mahy

3 Narrative outline

Students analyse the details of the story plot using a series of prompts. Use the photocopy master PM 14 on page 87. The same outline could be used to plan their own narrative writing or compare two stories.

STUDENT OUTCOMES
- Teaching the specific language features of narrative writing
- Developing comprehension through in-depth reading

Narrative outline

Your name: Sara Metz

Title Danny the Champion of the world

Author Roald Dahl

Illustrator Quentin Blake

Genre Adventure

Main characters Danny, William, Mr Victor Hazell and Doc Spencer

Setting Hazell wood and the filling station.

Situation Danny has turned nine and his father (William) frequently goes out poaching.

The problem Mr Victor Hazell is having a shooting party soon. Danny and his father want to spoil it. Because they don't want him to kill the pheasants.

Complications
- There are keepers armed with guns.
- William has a broken ankle.
- The pheasants can fly so they are quite hard to catch.
- It was hard to think of a way to give the pheasants the pills.

How does the story end? Danny and William save the pheasants. Then the pheasants wake from the sleeping pills and fly away so they are safe.

Based on *Danny, the Champion of the World* by Roald Dahl

4 Book review

Students comment on a book using a set of predetermined criteria. The teacher and class could develop a series of prompts for the students to use, especially if the book review will be given orally at some stage. Capable students could prepare their own list of criteria under which to assess the book. Class sets of book reviews could be kept in a clear file for students to use as a reference. Use the photocopy master PM 15 on page 88.

STUDENT OUTCOMES
- Developing evaluation skills such as assessing, justifying, recommending and rating
- Raising awareness of particular authors, illustrators and genre

---

Book review

Reviewer: *Adam*

Title: *Danny the Champion of the World*

Author: *Roald Dahl*

Illustrator: *Quentin Blake*

Fiction ✓   Non-fiction ☐   Genre *Adventure*

Main characters:

Danny *Danny's father (William)* *Doc Spencer* *Mr Victor Hazell*
Mrs Clipstone *Sergeant Enoch Samways* *Mr Rabbets*

Synopsis of story/text

It's a story about Danny and his father trying to save the pheasants, from Victor Hazell who wants to shoot them.

This illustration shows the part I enjoyed the most which was when *Danny drove the baby Austin.*

I recommend / ~~do not recommend~~ this book to others because *When Danny's left at home he always figures out what to do, whenever you stop reading the book you want to carry on.*

Based on *Danny, the Champion of the World* by Roald Dahl

---

5 Book assignment

Students individually complete a set of tasks within a prescribed time frame. Use the photocopy master PM 16 on page 89 for the 'Myths and legends book assignment' below. Book assignments are an excellent way of encouraging independence and providing opportunities for student choice. More capable students may be able to set their own book assignments once they become familiar with the types of tasks that are appropriate. Having groups of students working on book assignments has the added advantage of releasing the teacher to work with individuals or small groups.

Book assignments may be specific to a particular text or can be generic and used for a number of different texts.

Here are some ideas for generic book assignments:
- Myths and legends
- Characterisation
- Favourite author
- Poetry
- Short stories

PM 16

Myths and legends book assignment

Read this book assignment carefully. Choose either an A, B or C grade assignment to complete. Apart from activity 7, all parts of the book assignment must be completed individually unless negotiated with the teacher.

- Grade A: You must read *five* myths and legends and complete *five* activities.
- Grade B: You must read *four* myths and legends and complete *four* activities.
- Grade C: You must read *three* myths and legends and complete *three* activities.

☑ 1 Read a myth or legend, then complete a book review form about the story.

☑ 2 Find out more information about a hero, heroine, beast or mythical creature that appears in a myth or legend. Write a paragraph about what you found out. Draw a picture of the character and write three quotes from the story that describe the character's physical appearance.

☑ 3 Make a shoebox or triangle diorama to illustrate a part of one of the myths or legends you have read.

☐ 4 Ask your parents to tell you a myth or legend from a country where they or their ancestors came from (or visit the library and find out about one). Complete a storyboard of the events in the story and use it to retell the story to the class. Make a time with the teacher to do this.

☐ 5 Make a board game using your myth or legend as the theme.

☐ 6 Write a script for the story and present it as an overhead projector play.

☐ 7 Write a myth of your own to explain why a place or animal has certain features, for example, why the zebra has stripes. Use a narrative outline sheet to plan your story.

☐ 8 Rewrite a myth or legend as a Readers Theatre script that the class could perform. You may tell the original story or make up your own version.

I agree to complete a Grade ⃞C⃞ book assignment.

I agree to have my assignment completed by ___29 August___

Signed

Student: ___Jill Brown___

Teacher: ___Mrs Scott___   Date ___8 August___

6 Postcard

Postcards are 'mini letters' with specific language features. They are usually written when people are on holiday, don't include a lot of detailed information and usually don't require a response. Students could take on the role of one character writing to another character, real or imaginary, and have a friend reply to their postcard.

6 January 2003

Dear Grandma
We are having fun at Caramel Cove. Today it was really exciting because Dad and I were swimming and we saw a great white man-eating shark right beside us. Dad picked me up and ran as fast as he could to the beach. It was really scary but luckily the shark didn't get us. Dad says we are not allowed to go swimming again so it is a bit boring.

I hope you are well.

See you when we get home next week.

Love from Courtney xxx

Mrs Doris Dorsey
379 Te Moana Road
Waikanae

Based on *The Great White Man-Eating Shark* by Margaret Mahy.

7 Checklists

Students use the information in the text and their prior knowledge, if necessary, to write lists appropriate to the text. Suitable for both narrative and factual text.

Checklists

What to take for a day at Caramel Cove

swimsuit
towels
sunscreen
sun umbrella
picnic rug
drinks
lunch
bucket and spade
book to read

Stuff I need to make a fake shark fin belt

by Norvin
sheet of plastic
belt
scissors
tape

Based on *The Great White Man-Eating Shark* by Margaret Mahy.

8 Menus and recipes

Students design a menu for an occasion in their book, for example, a special afternoon tea for the grandmother in the story of *Little Red Riding Hood*. Specific recipes could be included.

Menu for Grandma's afternoon tea

Lemon & honey drink

Egg & cucumber sandwiches

Chocolate chip cookies

Sultana cake

9 Dialogue journal

Dialogue journals involve both the teacher and the student in a written dialogue about a given text. The teacher responds to the student's thoughts and ideas about the story and poses questions, comments and other points of view to help extend the student's thinking.

Dialogue journals can be written in response to picture books or as an ongoing activity while reading a novel. It is important to model the journal writing by providing question stems that will challenge and extend students' thinking. It is also vital that students receive regular response to their writing to show them their work is valued. Along with teacher feedback, this can be achieved by setting up discussion groups of three or more students to provide opportunities for them to share their thoughts and ideas. Initially, modelling the discussion in a larger group is necessary. This type of discussion is particularly appropriate for shared novel studies and is sometimes called literacy circles. It may be appropriate to write journals for only a specified period of time depending on the interest level of the students. It is important that journal writing is not seen as a 'chore' or a time filler.

The ideas for question stems illustrated could be photocopied onto sheets and glued to the inside cover of students' journal books. Students could also add their own ideas.

For more ideas for discussion see the 'Pick a card' activity on page 67 and related photocopy master PM 18 on pages 91–93.

What did you think was going to happen in the story?

If I was … I would have …

Why do you think the author wrote the book?

I noticed that…

Did you identify with any of the characters in the book? Explain why.

I thought the illustrations in this text/story were … because …

Was there a lesson to be learned from this book?

I am unclear about …

I was surprised when …

I felt the same way as … when …

The character that … reminded me of was … from the book … because …

I predicted that … but I was surprised when … because …

10 Get in touch! — writing responses

STUDENT OUTCOMES
- Developing personal connections with literature
- Creating authentic writing experiences

Students write a letter, fax or e-mail to:

- an author — author websites are a good place to find contact details; some publishing companies may forward mail to their authors
- find out more information about a particular topic raised in the story or text they have read
- express an opinion regarding an issue raised in the story or text.

AIRMAIL

Harry Price
West Wing Publishing Company
44–48 Cheshire Street
London SW10
England

11 Dust jacket

PM 17

STUDENT OUTCOMES
- Developing graphic skills such as font, layout, size and colour
- Building knowledge of, and preference for, particular authors

Students design a new dust jacket for the book. Discuss the features of a dust jacket, for example, title, name of author and illustrator, synopsis of story, author biography, reviews, and publisher's information, before attempting to create one. Use photocopy master PM 17 on page 90.

As this is a challenging task, pairs or small groups of students could work on different components of the dust jacket. These could then be collated. Dust jackets could also be designed for videotapes or CDs.

REVIEWS
"The most exciting adventure story I have ever read!" — Shakera, Room 15
"I kept wanting to read this book, it had so many exciting parts." — Sam, Room 20   5

Brian Robeson is flying to see his father. The plane he is travelling in crashes in the Canadian north woods after the pilot dies of a heart attack. Brian survives the crash but faces many more challenges in the isolated woods he has landed in. This is a survival story of how a boy from the city copes with living in a very different environment than he is used to.   6

ABOUT THE AUTHOR Gary Paulsen was born in Minnesota in the USA. He didn't do very well at school and tried many jobs before he became a magazine editor and then an author. He has written articles, short stories and plays but he is most famous for his novels.   7

HATCHET by GARY PAULSEN
PUFFIN BOOKS   4

HATCHET   1

2

GARY PAULSEN   3

Based on *Hatchet* by Gary Paulsen

12 Author or illustrator biography

STUDENT OUTCOMES
• Developing scanning skills
• Building knowledge of, and preference for, particular authors

Students research information on a particular author or illustrator and write a biography. Library databases and publisher and author websites are good places to find information. In addition to the biography, the students could compile a list of other titles written by the same author. If writing about an illustrator, the student could also create an illustration in the style of that illustrator. Eric Carle, Ann Jonas, Chris van Allsburg and Jeannie Baker would be suitable illustrators for this task.

A class collection of biographies could be kept in a clear file folder for students to use as a reference.

Margaret Mahy
by Sophie Villers

13 Facts and opinions

STUDENT OUTCOMES
• Developing personal responses to ideas in the text
• Developing ability to distinguish between fact and opinion

Students list a number of facts from the story. Underneath each fact they write an opinion that relates to that fact. As an introduction to this concept the teacher could make a game where facts and opinions were written on strips of card. The students could match the fact with the opinion.

Facts and opinions

Title of book: Amos and Boris   **Author:** William Steig

Your name: Sam

Fact: Amos built his own boat and went sailing alone	
Opinion: It was dangerous to sail by himself	

Fact: Amos fell off his boat soon after his adventure started and was saved by Boris
Opinion: If Amos had not met Boris he would have drowned

Fact: Amos and Boris became very close friends
Opinion: Amos and Boris' lives were enriched by their chance meeting

Fact: Boris thought Amos would never be able to help him
Opinion: Amos was a wiser animal than Boris

Based on *Amos and Boris* by William Steig

Your ideas

Chapter 6

Organising for talk

Other responses that include talking are:

- The hot seat: character interview
- Book discussions when students are involved in writing dialogue journals
- Television or radio news item
- Advertisement
- Book review
- Conversations

The following responses are useful frameworks for orally retelling the story or text:

- Timeline
- Flow chart
- Wall story
- Circular story
- Storyboard
- Sequencing pictures or text
- Excitement chart
- Story map
- Board game
- Narrative outline
- Overhead projector play
- Prop box
- Readers Theatre
- Read and retell

1 True, false, I'm not sure

The teacher writes a series of statements based on the text. Some of the statements are factual and can be found in the text. Other statements require the students to use their prior knowledge and think beyond the information contained in the text. In pairs or in a small group, the students discuss whether the statements fit into one of three categories, true, false or I'm not sure. They must come to a consensus and be able to support their ideas.

YES! this is true	**NO!** this is not true ... it's a big lie	**?** I'm not sure
Sharks eat fish	A shark would make a good pet	Sharks can live in rivers
Sharks can eat people	Sharks do not have teeth	People eat sharks
Sharks live in the sea	Sharks are the biggest sea animal	You should not kill sharks

2 Book 'selling'

Students give an oral presentation to promote a book they have enjoyed. Teacher and students co-operatively set up a structure for students to follow to ensure they cover a range of information about the book. This could include a combination of the following: author, illustrator, genre, brief synopsis of book, recommendation rating, the sharing of a response such as a diorama the student has made for the book if appropriate, a brief reading to encourage other children to read the book, and links to other texts.

A prompt chart or hand-held laminated card could serve to remind the speaker of areas to cover.

3 Overhead projector play

STUDENT OUTCOMES
- **Strengthening co-operative learning skills**
- **Creating opportunities for rereading the text to encourage fluency**

Students draw and cut out characters from light card or overhead transparency paper. Glue or tape a popsicle stick or similar to the back of the character so it can be manoeuvred across the screen. Background scenes can be drawn on overhead transparency sheets. Black line drawings are sufficient, as colouring in background scenes can become messy and time consuming. Scripts and puppets can be stored in resealable plastic bags and used as an independent reading activity.

4 Who am I?

STUDENT OUTCOMES
- **Developing descriptive writing skills**
- **Building knowledge of literature**

Students write a brief description of a character, and other members of the group try to guess who it is. This idea can be used as a starter activity for the reading session. Have the whole class write a 'Who am I?' and put them into a box. Students take turns to read them out and other students try to guess who the character is. An alternative to this could be to read a quote from a particular character and have the students guess who said it and when it was said.

Who am I?

I live in a forest with *my* parents. My family enjoys going for morning walks. Porridge is *my* favourite breakfast.

5 Barrier games

STUDENT OUTCOMES
- Developing speaking and listening skills
- Encouraging co-operative learning skills

Barrier games are especially useful for second language learners to encourage oral language and listening skills. There are many variations of barrier games but the basic idea is that two students sit opposite each other with a barrier in between them (a large open book is usually sufficient). Commonly both children have the same picture, for instance six clowns wearing six different outfits. One partner describes one clown and the other partner has to guess which one it is. A variation is for the partners to be given the same picture with slight differences. They have to ask each other questions to establish what the differences are. Another variation on this is to have one partner describe a simple drawing and the other partner draws it. Much of the teaching value from this activity comes from the discussion after the activity. The listener is often blamed if the picture is drawn incorrectly but research shows that it is usually the fault of the partner describing the picture.

6 Which came first?

STUDENT OUTCOMES
- Facilitating rereading of the text to promote understanding
- Developing the ability to substantiate statements

The teacher copies two sentences from the story onto one piece of card. Make a set of ten cards or more depending on the size of the group. The students work in pairs, each taking turns to decide which event occurred first in the story. They must substantiate their thinking by going back into the text.

The mouse tells the Gruffalo he is the scariest creature in the world.

The Gruffalo meets the snake.

Owl invites the mouse to lunch in his treetop house.

Owl meets the Gruffalo.

Mouse says the Gruffalo's favourite food is roasted fox.

The Gruffalo runs away from the mouse.

Based on *The Gruffalo* by Julia Donaldson

7 Question cards

The teacher makes a set of six cards containing the question starters 'Who?', 'When?', 'Why?', 'Where?', 'What?' and 'How?'. After students have read the text, they are each given a card; two students may have to share a card if there are more than six in a group. The students have to formulate a question using the prompt card they have. Students take turns to ask a question beginning with the prompt they have. Other students answer the questions. Model the use of open-ended questions that extend thinking, such as 'What would you have done if you had been Jack?', rather than closed questions such as 'What did Jack do when the boys bullied him?'

Question cards

Who are the main characters in this story/text?
When did this story/text take place?
Why did the characters do the things they did?
Where did this story/text take place?
What are the main events/problems/issues in this story/text?
How do the author and illustrator use visual language?

8 Prop box

Students use props to retell a story, represent a character or develop an innovation on text.

Ideas for a prop box:
Hats, scarves, wigs, gloves, mirror, comb, sunglasses, tickets, bunch of artificial flowers, shell, puppets, fabric scraps (a piece of blue fabric could represent the sea), old camera, keys, shoes, small box, and so on.

9 Readers Theatre

Readers Theatre is a form of choral reading. Groups of students present a piece of literature by reading aloud from hand-held scripts. Readers Theatre scripts can be developed from original literature, such as plays, poems, stories or excerpts from stories, or students can write their own scripts or innovate on known texts. A group of students are assigned a particular character or part of the text that they read in unison. All students have a copy of the script and readers are not expected to memorise their parts. Colour-coding parts can be helpful to younger students. A pair or group of students are assigned the role of the narrator. Use of costumes is not necessary and there is little physical movement. The focus is on the facial expressions, gestures and vocal inflections of the readers.

There is much value in students reading and rereading the text. The anticipation of performance is highly motivating. Expressive reading, fluency and understandings about characters can be greatly improved by regular sessions of Readers Theatre.

10 Practised reading

Student choose a particular passage of the text that appeals to them. This could be an extract from a picture or poetry book or a novel or short story. The reading should be no less than a paragraph and no more than a page. Students rehearse the reading and present it to the class, explaining why they have chosen it. Students could dress as a character in the story if they wished.

11 'Pick a card' activity

PM 18

The cards are designed to encourage purposeful focused discussion and critical thinking. Use the photocopy master PM 18 on pages 91–93. These pages can be enlarged to A3 size, backed with cardboard and cut out. The teacher selects appropriate cards for specific modelling to small groups. It is important to create a supportive atmosphere where students feel safe to respond. Encourage the students to join in by passing around the same card for everyone who wants to have a turn. The group needs to support each student by encouraging him or her to go further and deeper into his or her response each time the activity is completed. The cards can be the basis for developing more extensive responses and reactions leading to fuller group discussion. Individual students can choose a card from the selection available that day. While these cards have been designed for co-operative oral discussion, they can be used successfully for written responses following discussion.

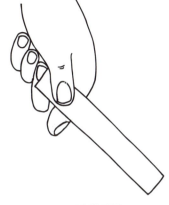

In the beginning this text talked about … then … finally

The most useful diagram/picture/graph was … because …

The main ideas in this text/story were … and …

In my own words this story/text is about …

Developed by John McCaffery

12 Sequencing text — confirm with tape

The teacher condenses the story into a shorter version. The story is then typed out and divided into strips that can be cut out. Cut strips and put each set of story strips into envelopes or resealable plastic bags.

Students work in pairs to co-operatively order the strips into a sequence that makes sense. The teacher then plays a taped version of the story. Audio cassette tapes are provided with some books or can be made by the teacher. Students listen to the tape and confirm or change order if necessary.

Amos decides to build himself a boat and go sailing to see the world.

He provisions the boat with food, equipment and other necessities.

With all his strength, Amos pushes his boat into the water and sets sail.

One night, he accidentally falls off his boat and lands in the ocean.

He spends a very frightening night alone in the water.

Just when he is preparing to die, he meets a friendly whale called Boris.

He asks Boris to take him back to land and the whale agrees to help.

On the way to land the animals become friends and sadly say goodbye.

Years later, a hurricane strikes and Boris is left stranded on the beach.

Coincidentally Amos finds Boris and desperately tries to save him.

He asks two elephants to push Boris back into the water, which they do.

Their friendship cemented for ever, the two friends sadly say goodbye.

Based on *Amos and Boris* by William Steig

13 Read and retell

Although this procedure is probably more suited to being a whole class activity, it may also be used in a small group situation.

1 The teacher chooses a short story or passage of text.
2 Students work with a partner.
3 The teacher tells the students the title and asks them to predict what the story will be about and what words they might expect to see in the story.
4 The teacher asks them to discuss their prediction and words with their partner.
5 The teacher reads the story through twice, then asks the students to write down the story as closely as possible to the original version.
6 Partners then discuss their retellings with each other.

Instead of the teacher reading aloud the passage or story, students may read the passage a number of times themselves before reconstructing the story in written form or orally to a partner. This method would be more suitable for when the teacher is working with a number of reading groups in the classroom. There is much value in repeating this procedure a number of times over time using a variety of different text types, both factual and narrative. Students may keep samples of their retellings to check improvement over time.

The Selfish Giant
When they were coming home the children would play in the giants garden. There were flowers that looked like stars and there were twelve peach trees. In Autunm they would have blossoms growing and in Spring fruit. The birds would sing beutifully, the children would stop playing to listen. One day the giant came back from Cornish ogres house where he stayed for seven years. When he saw the children he yelled After that he built a wall with a sign saying tresspassers will be prosacuted.

Based on *The Selfish Giant* by Oscar Wilde

14 Conversations

The teacher recounts situations that occur in the text that would inspire conversation. The situations could be written on cards and stored in resealable plastic bags to be used again. Students work in pairs or small groups to construct a conversation that might have occurred in a situation from the story. The conversation is written in script form and then performed to the whole class.

Conversations

Write a script for a conversation that could have occurred in these situations:

Boris discovers Amos alone in the middle of the ocean.

(2 people)

Amos and Boris meet after Boris has been washed up on the beach after the hurricane.

(2 people)

A frantic Amos comes upon two elephants walking near the beach after Hurricane Yetta.

(3 people)

Swimming out to sea, Boris encounters two of his whale friends after Amos and the elephants save him.

(3 people)

Based on *Amos and Boris* by William Steig

Your ideas

Bibliography

Referenced titles

Baker, Jeannie, *Window*. Random House, London, 1991.

Beck, Jennifer, *The Bantam and the Soldier*. Scholastic Publishers, Auckland, 1996.

Blume, Judy, *Fudgemania,* Bodley Head, London, 1991.

———, *Superfudge*, Bodley Head, London, 1991.

Briggs, Raymond, *Jim and the Beanstalk*. Puffin Picture Books, London, 1970.

Carian, Douglas, *The First Olympic Marathon*. School Journal, Part 4, Number 1, 1996, Learning Media, Wellington, 1996.

Dahl, Roald, *Danny, the Champion of the World*. Jonathan Cape, London, 1994.

Donaldson, Julia, *The Gruffalo*. Koala Books, New South Wales, 1999.

Grace, Patricia, *The Kuia and the Spider*. Penguin, Auckland, 1981.

Mahy, Margaret, *The Great White Man-Eating Shark*. Penguin Books, London, 1989.

Milne, A.A., *Winnie The Pooh*. Methuen, London, 1977.

Paulsen, Gary, *Hatchet*. Aladdin Paperbacks, New York, 1996.

Potter, Beatrix, *The Tale of Peter Rabbit*. Frederick Warne, London,1987.

Shannon, Gillian, *Plants that Store Water*. School Journal, Part 2, Number 3, 1993, Learning Media, Wellington, 1993.

Steig, William, *Amos and Boris*. Farrar, Straus and Giroux, New York, 1971.

Taylor, William, *Crash! The story of Poddy*. Scholastic Publishers, Auckland, 2000.

Tolkien, J.R.R., *The Hobbit*. Unwin Books, London, 1966.

Van Allsburg, Chris, *The Polar Express*. Anderson Press, Boston, 1985.

Wilde, Oscar, *The Fairy Tales of Oscar Wilde*. Henry Hill and Company, Inc, New York, 1993.

Wilson, Jacqueline, *Bad Girls*. Corgi Yearling Books, London, 1996.

Zion, Gene, *Harry the Dirty Dog*. Random House, London, 1992.

Other titles

Brown, Hazel, and Brian Cambourne, *Read and Retell*. Methuen, North Ryde, New South Wales, 1987.

De Bono, Edward, *Teaching Thinking*. Temple Smith, London, 1976.

Dymock, Susan, and Tom Nicholson, *Reading Comprehension: What is it? How do you teach it?* NZCER, Wellington, 1999.

Hill, Susan, *Readers Theatre: Performing the Text*. Eleanor Curtain Publishing, South Yarra, Victoria, 1990.

Johnson, Terry D., and Daphne R. Louis, *Literacy through Literature*. Methuen, North Ryde, New South Wales, 1985.

Nicoll, Vivienne, and Victoria Roberts, *Taking a Closer Look at Literature-Based Programs*. Primary English Teaching Association, Newton, New South Wales, 1993.

Articles

Gambrell, L. Creating cultures that foster reading motivation, *The Reading Teacher*, (50) 1, 1996: 14–25.

Gambrell, L., B. Martin-Palmer, R.M. Codling and S. Anders-Mazzoni. Assessing motivation to read, *The Reading Teacher*, (49) 7, 1996: 518–533.

Hancock, M.R. Exploring and extending personal response through literature journals, *The Reading Teacher*, (46) 6, 1993: 466–473.

Martinez M., N.L. Roser and S. Strecker. "I never thought I could be a star": A Readers Theatre ticket to fluency, *The Reading Teacher*, (52) 4, 1999: 326–334.

Short, K., G. Kauffman and L.H. Kahn. I just need to draw: Responding to literature across multiple sign systems. *The Reading Teacher,* (54) 2, 2000: 160–171.

Spiegel, D.L. Reader response approaches and the growth of readers, *Language Arts,* (76) 1, 1998: 41–46.

Turner, J., and S.J. Paris. How literacy tasks influence children's motivation for literacy, *The Reading Teacher,* (48) 8, 1995: 662–672.

Photocopy masters

Y chart

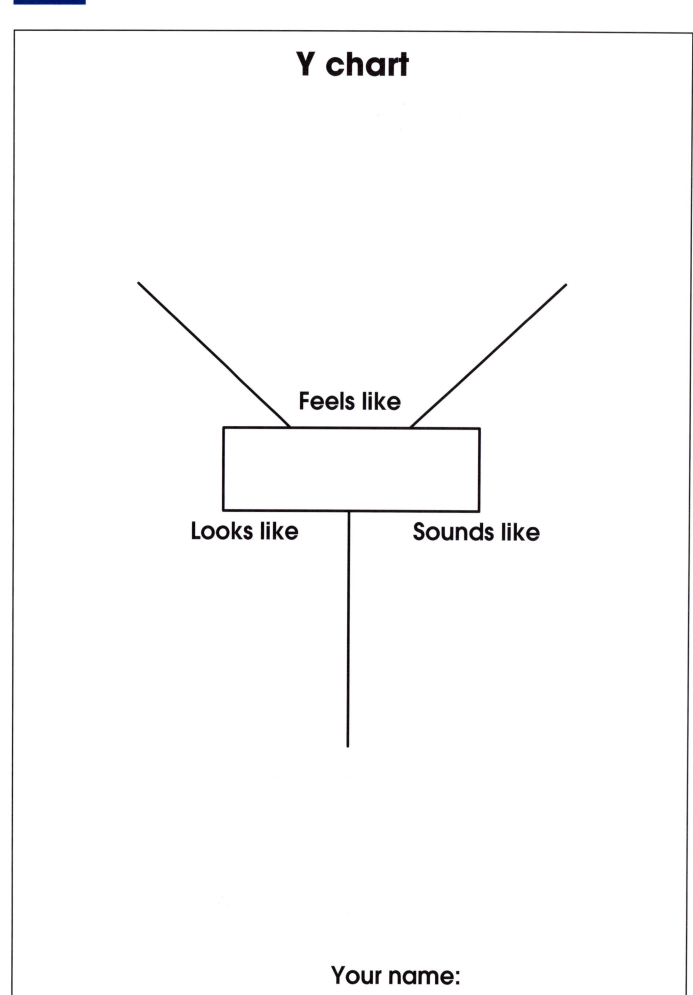

Feels like

Looks like   **Sounds like**

Your name:

Storyboard for

Your name

Title:

Author:

1	3	5
2	4	6
		7
		8

PMI chart for:

Your name:

PLUS	MINUS	INTERESTING

Predict and check chart

Your name:

Title and author	Word	Page	Your definition	Expert definition

Word search for

Author:

Created by:

Completed by:

Your name:

Venn diagram for

Title:

Author:

Time in story:

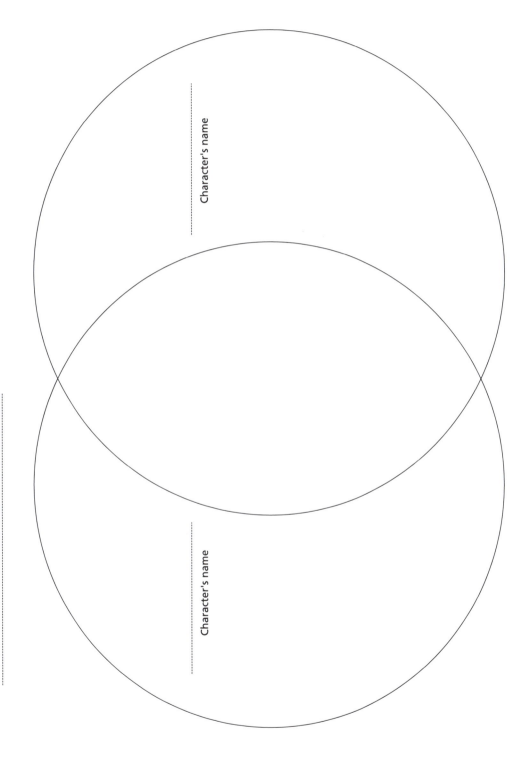

Character's name

Character's name

Character grid organiser for:

Your name: _____

Character	Physical appearance	Personal characteristics

Character web

Your name: ....

Title: ....

Author: ....

Illustrator: ....

Character: ....

Time in story: ....

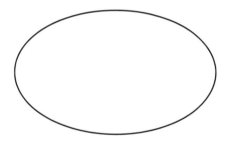

Character rating chart

Story: .... **Your name:** ....

Author: ....

Time in story: ....

Adjective	Character				Justification

The Reading Activity Handbook, published 2004 by Collins © Sheena Cameron, Reed Publishing (NZ), 2004.

Character book assignment

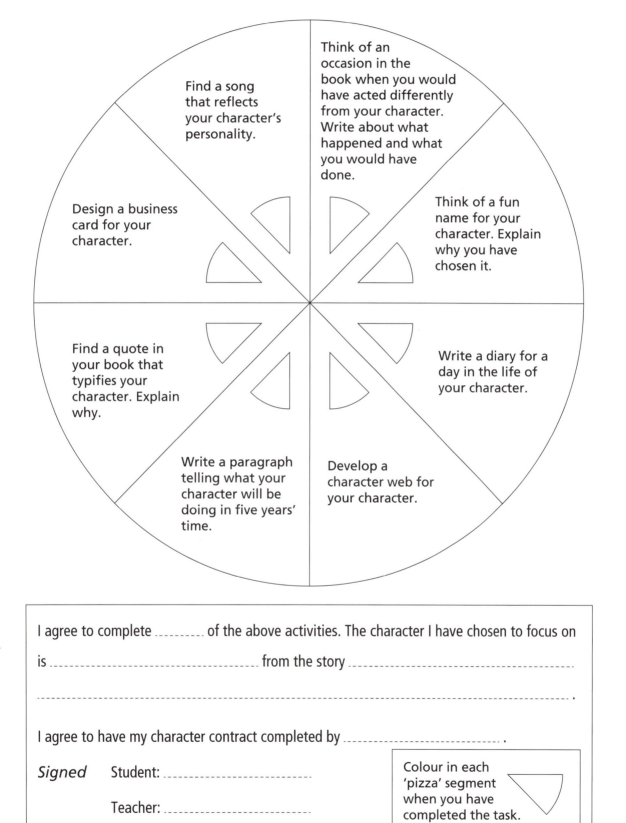

Find a song that reflects your character's personality.

Think of an occasion in the book when you would have acted differently from your character. Write about what happened and what you would have done.

Design a business card for your character.

Think of a fun name for your character. Explain why you have chosen it.

Find a quote in your book that typifies your character. Explain why.

Write a diary for a day in the life of your character.

Write a paragraph telling what your character will be doing in five years' time.

Develop a character web for your character.

I agree to complete _____ of the above activities. The character I have chosen to focus on

is _____ from the story _____

_____ .

I agree to have my character contract completed by _____ .

Signed   Student: _____

Teacher: _____

Date: _____

Colour in each 'pizza' segment when you have completed the task.

Bad luck cards :(

Rules

Good luck cards :)

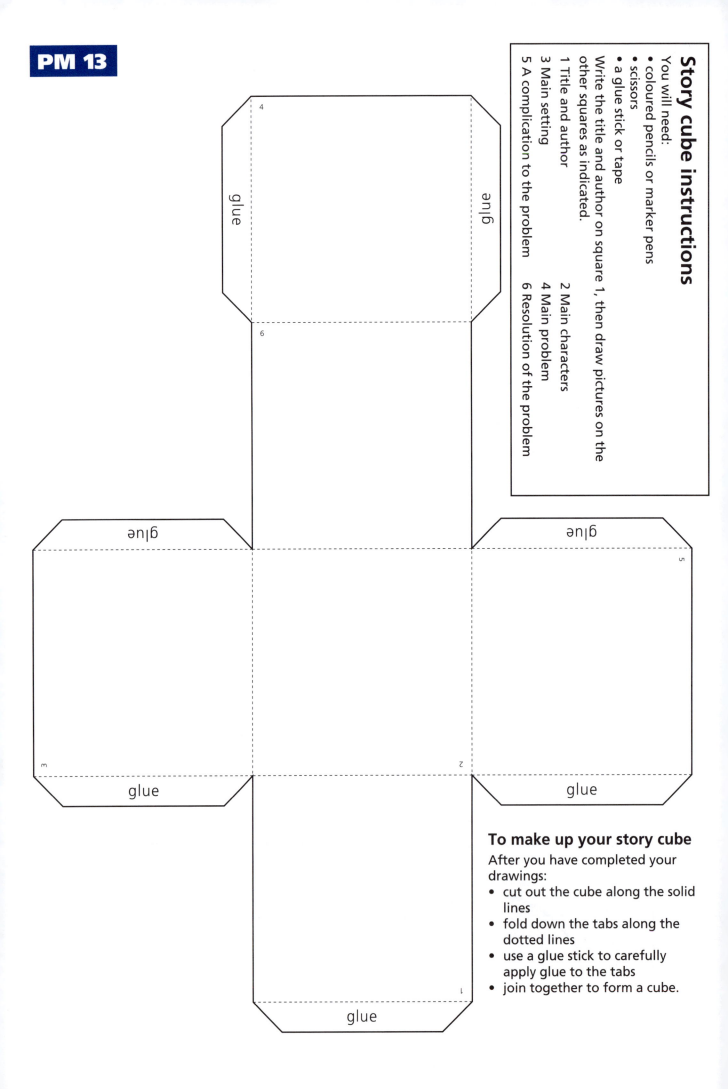

Story cube instructions

You will need:
- coloured pencils or marker pens
- scissors
- a glue stick or tape

Write the title and author on square 1, then draw pictures on the other squares as indicated.

1 Title and author
2 Main characters
3 Main setting
4 Main problem
5 A complication to the problem
6 Resolution of the problem

glue

glue

glue

glue

glue

glue

glue

To make up your story cube

After you have completed your drawings:
- cut out the cube along the solid lines
- fold down the tabs along the dotted lines
- use a glue stick to carefully apply glue to the tabs
- join together to form a cube.

Narrative outline

Your name:

Title

Author

Illustrator

Genre

Main characters

Setting

Situation

The problem

Complications

How does the story end?

Book review

Reviewer: _____

Title: _____

Author: _____

Illustrator: _____

Fiction ☐   Non-fiction ☐   Genre _____

Main characters:

Synopsis of story/text

This illustration shows the part I enjoyed the most which was when

I recommend / do not recommend this book to others because

The Reading Activity Handbook, published 2004 by Collins © Sheena Cameron, Reed Publishing (NZ), 2004.
This page may be photocopied for use in the classroom.

Myths and legends book assignment

Read this book assignment carefully. Choose either an A, B or C grade assignment to complete. Apart from activity 7, all parts of the book assignment must be completed individually unless negotiated with the teacher.

- Grade A: You must read *five* myths and legends and complete *five* activities.
- Grade B: You must read *four* myths and legends and complete *four* activities.
- Grade C: You must read *three* myths and legends and complete *three* activities.

❑ 1 Read a myth or legend, then complete a book review form about the story.

❑ 2 Find out more information about a hero, heroine, beast or mythical creature that appears in a myth or legend. Write a paragraph about what you found out. Draw a picture of the character and write three quotes from the story that describe the character's physical appearance.

❑ 3 Make a shoebox or triangle diorama to illustrate a part of one of the myths or legends you have read.

❑ 4 Ask your parents to tell you a myth or legend from a country where they or their ancestors came from (or visit the library and find out about one). Complete a storyboard of the events in the story and use it to retell the story to the class. Make a time with the teacher to do this.

❑ 5 Make a board game using your myth or legend as the theme.

❑ 6 Write a script for the story and present it as an overhead projector play.

❑ 7 Write a myth of your own to explain why a place or animal has certain features, for example, why the zebra has stripes. Use a narrative outline sheet to plan your story.

❑ 8 Rewrite a myth or legend as a Readers Theatre script that the class could perform. You may tell the original story or make up your own version.

I agree to complete a Grade ❑ book assignment.

I agree to have my assignment completed by _____

Signed

Student: _____

Teacher: _____   Date _____

1

2

3

4

5

6

7

8

Dust jacket key: 1 title **2** illustration **3** author/illustrator **4** title/author/publisher **5** reviews **6** synopsis of story **7** about the author **8** picture of author

'Pick a card' discussion stems

Understanding the text

In the beginning this text talked about … then … finally …

The most useful diagram/picture/graph was … because …

The main ideas in this text/story were … and …

In my own words this story/text is about …

Finding the viewpoints

The author's viewpoint in this text/story is …

In my opinion a viewpoint in this text story is …

This picture/illustration shows that …

How the viewpoint is expressed by the text

This picture/illustration on page … shows that …

The way the author uses words on page … shows that …

Other viewpoints in the text/story can be seen/found in …

Where this viewpoint comes from

I think the author/illustrator believes that … because …

I think this viewpoint comes from …

A viewpoint similar to/different from this is …

Other places this viewpoint can be found are …

The audience this text was written for was … because …

The Reading Activity Handbook, published 2004 by Collins © Sheena Cameron, Reed Publishing (NZ), 2004.
This page may be photocopied for use in the classroom.

'Pick a card' discussion stems (cont.)

Expressing your own viewpoint/experience

I thought this was a good text/story because …

I felt … when … because …

I like the part when … because …

When I look at this picture/illustration it makes me feel …

When I read this book/text I thought about …

Other sources of information

Other places I might find information on this viewpoint are …

I think this is a good/poor source of information because …

People I could ask about this viewpoint are …

My personal experience of this viewpoint is …

One thing I would like to know more about is … My family would say that …

Comparing and contrasting viewpoints

The author's viewpoint is … My viewpoint is …

I agree/disagree with the author because …

Another author's viewpoint on this is …

The text/story says that … I agree/disagree because …

A word/phrase I was unsure of was … I think it meant …

'Pick a card' discussion stems (cont.)

Critiquing and justifying

The text/story made me think about … because …

This is a good/poor source of information because …

I agree/disagree with this viewpoint because …

My opinion is …

I think that …

I would like to say that …

My feeling is …

Social action implications

A new ending for this story/text could be …

If I was … I could …

This viewpoint is relevant to my life because …

I could explore this viewpoint further by …

We could …

I think …

If I had the power to … I would … because …

Other people who could help are …

Descriptive words chart

HAPPY

aglow	close	exuberant	high-spirited	lively	silly
airy	comfortable	exultant	hilarious	merry	sparkling
animated	contented	festive	inspired	mirthful	spirited
blissful	debonair	frisky	jaunty	peaceful	sunny
blithe	delighted	gay	jolly	playful	thankful
bright	ecstatic	genial	jovial	pleased	thrilled
brisk	elated	giddy	joyful	rapturous	tranquil
bubbly	enthusiastic	glad	joyous	satisfied	uplifted
cheerful	euphoric	gleeful	jubilant	saucy	vivacious
cheery	exhilarated	grateful	lighthearted	serene	warm

SAD

blue	despondent	downcast	glum	morose	spiritless
cheerless	disconsolate	downhearted	grief-stricken	mournful	sullen
choked up	discontented	dreadful	hollow	oppressed	sympathetic
clouded	discouraged	dull	joyless	out of sorts	unhappy
dark	disheartened	empty	melancholy	quiet	woebegone
dejected	dismal	flat	miserable	sombre	woeful
depressed	doleful	gloomy	moping	sorrowful	wretched

FEARLESS

audacious	certain	dauntless	hardy	plucky	strong
bold	confident	determined	heroic	resolute	unafraid
brave	courageous	firm	independent	secure	valiant
calm	daring	gallant	intrepid	self-reliant	valorous

AFRAID

aghast	cautious	faint-hearted	immobilised	restless	terror-stricken
alarmed	chicken	fearful	insecure	scared	threatened
anxious	cowardly	fidgety	intimidated	shaky	timid
appalled	craven	frightened	nervous	sheepish	timorous
apprehensive	diffident	hesitant	panicky	shocked	tremulous
awed	dismayed	horrified	paralysed	suspicious	worried
breathless	doubtful	hysterical	petrified	terrified	yellow

EAGER

anxious	avid	desirous	enthusiastic	intent	willing
ardent	bursting	earnest	fervent	keen	zealous

DOUBTFUL

cautious	distant	hesitant	perplexed	suspicious	unconvinced
cynical	distrustful	incredulous	questioning	unbelieving	unsure
disbelieving	dubious	indecisive	sceptical	uncertain	wavering

INTERESTED

absorbed	captivated	curious	excited	inquisitive	nosy
affected	concerned	engrossed	fascinated	intrigued	riveted

HURT

aching	crushed	heartbroken	mournful	rueful	victimised
afflicted	distressed	injured	offended	sore	woeful
aggrieved	embarrassed	in despair	pathetic	tortured	worried
agonised	hapless	in pain	piteous	upset	wounded

ANGRY

aggravated	critical	fuming	in a stew	offended	sulky
agitated	cross	furious	irate	outraged	sullen
annoyed	defiant	heated	irked	piqued	up in arms
belligerent	enraged	incensed	irritated	provoked	vexed
bitter	exasperated	indignant	livid	resentful	wild
boiling	fed up	inflamed	mad	riled	worked up
contemptuous	fiery	infuriated	miffed	seething	wrathful

MISCELLANEOUS

affectionate	disillusioned	hysterical	powerless	seductive	sweaty
bewildered	dominant	jealous	proud	soft	talkative
complacent	encouraged	loving	reassured	submissive	tired
dependent	envious	nauseated	respectful	surprised	tolerant

Notes

Notes